The Wurzels

Somerset Cider Walks

Your Guide to Some
Of The Best
Cider Walks In Somerset

The Wurzels

Somerset Cider Walks

Your Guide to Some Of The Best Cider Walks In Somerset

Glen Board

Somerset Valley Publishing

Published in the UK by:

Somerset Valley Publishing Ltd

1 Tenterk Close,

Bleadon, BS24 0PJ

England, UK

First Published 2019

Copyright © Glen Board

ISBN 978-1-9160011-2-1

Note:

The author and publisher do not accept any responsibility or liability for loss or injury arising from the use or misuse of any of the information contained in this book.

In Memory of Adge Cutler...

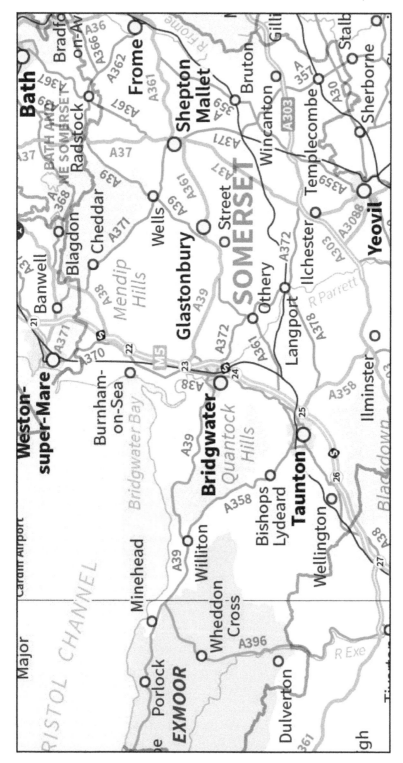

Map Showing the Beautiful County of Somerset

Contents

- A Brief History of The Wurzels   page 9

- Cider Making in Somerset   page 12

- Walk 1 - The Bleadon to Uphill Round Robin   page 17

- Roger Wilkins - The Cider King!   page 32

- Walk 2 - Mudgley to Godney Apple Cart Race   page 34

- The Cider Barn   page 43

- Walk 3 - The Priddy Cider Press Circular   page 44

- Thatchers Cider - Somerset Cider at its Heart   page 54

- Walk 4 - The Minehead to Porlock Apple Taster   page 56

- Rich's Farmhouse Cider   page 63

- Walk 5 - The Porlock Weir Knee Trembler   page 66

- Hecks Farmhouse Cider   page 76

- Walk 6 - The East to West Harptree Full Flagon   page 78

- Hedgers Cider   page 86

- Walk 7 - The Blagdon Lake, Leg Thrasher   page 89

- Tucker's Grave Inn   page 100

- Wassailing at Rich's Cider   page 101

Somerset

Photography Credits

The images on pages 53 and 54 are courtesy and Copyright © Thatchers Cider.
Front and rear cover images of the apple orchard are courtesy and Copyright © Thatchers Cider.

All images of The Aplin family are courtesy of Frank Aplin.

All images of The Wurzels are courtesy and Copyright © Michael Pelling.

The image of Glastonbury Tor (page 42) and the Apple Orchard (page 15) are courtesy of Steve Bradford.

Miller's at the Anchor in Porlock Weir: cc-by-sa/2.0 © Steve Daniels geograph.org.uk/p/3520328.

The Anchor in Porlock Weir: cc-by-sa- © Philip-Halling geograph/p/1400462.

The Royal Oak in High Street: cc-by-sa/2.0 - © Basher Eyre - geograph.org.uk/p/933714.

The Old Ship Aground: cc-by-sa/2.0 © M J Richardson - geograph.org.uk/p/3738361.

The Ship Inn in Porlock Weir: cc-by-sa/2.0 - © Steve Daniels - geograph.org.uk/p/3506227.

Images of Tucker's Grave Inn on page 100 are courtesy of Jo Watts.

Images of Wassailing at Rich's Cider on page 101 are courtesy of Oliver Woolacott.

All other photography in this book Copyright © Glen Board.

All of the illustrations are by Jordan Skidmore.

A Brief History of The Wurzels

The Wurzels are without doubt one of the best known and loved bands to come out of Somerset and indeed the whole of the United Kingdom. Many of us will remember growing up and listening to their amazingly catchy tunes while our parents drank a nice pint of cider and enjoyed the long hot summers which we used to be blessed with back in the 1960's and 70's.

It all started with the legendary character of Adge Cutler whose unique style was formed from a childhood which was blessed to be in the Somerset of a by-gone age. Adge was born in the town of

Pete Budd

Portishead back in 1931 but spent his youth growing up in the nearby town of Nailsea, where he would often venture out into the nearby countryside and see the farming which was going on all around.

As we all know 'round these parts, farming is deeply entwined with the wonderful Somerset culture of making cider from our ancient apple orchards which are littered all around the county - and as with many of us who have grown up in this most beautiful of counties, the young Adge was soon to be tasting the delights of our very own nectar from heaven!

Tommy Banner

Proud of their roots, a deep interest in local folklore, and with a keen interest in music and cider, this now became a unique melting pot which formed The Wurzels into a talent which was to hit deep into the hearts of many generations to come.

A few people have come and gone over the years but the band is still going strong with the current line-up consisting of Pete Budd, Tommy Banner, John

John Morgan

Morgan and Sedge Moore, and they are still touring with a busy schedule – see the website www.thewurzels.com for all current information on The Wurzels.

Sedge Moore

The witty lyrics and songs which have come from the band over the past five decades have been phenomenal, and the impact that they have had on the county has been unprecedented – they are truly 'legends in their own lifetimes' and are fondly talked about throughout the old Pubs, Inns and Cider Farms of this old and stunning county. In fact, the word 'Wurzels' and 'Cider' have become so entwined that to your local cider drinker they are both terms to be very proud of and loved.

In this book we would like to present to you a guide as to how you can get out and enjoy some of the pleasure that 'us locals' have all had over the years while drinking the 'local brew' in our gorgeous Somerset (Zomerzet in the local tongue).

We will describe to you, how you can get out in beautiful Somerset and enjoy a day's walk, and at the same time enjoy a few pints of cider along the way. Many of our best pubs and cider houses are tucked out of the way, so will not be obvious to many tourists and indeed some locals as to their existence. However, within the pages of this book we will guide you to some of our favourite drinking spots – so lace up your walking boots, dust off your maps and get yourself out into Somerset's stunning countryside, and of course make sure that you have a nice cold pint of cider or two along the way!

Cider Making in Somerset

Somerset is without doubt the Cider Capital of the World, with other English counties or even worse, foreign countries now trying to jump on our apple cart. There has been something of a resurgence of the popularity of cider in recent years with many now seeing it as a trendy drink to sup with their friends, which can sometimes be seen to parallel the culture that emerged out of the 1980's 'yuppie era' with wine drinking.

However, here in Somerset things have always been different and for hundreds, if not thousands of years we have always loved our very own gold elixir – keeping it secret to outsiders who would scoff at our regional heritage and more importantly couldn't handle its effects. This is especially true when they are introduced to our traditional farmhouse varieties of Scrumpy which always seem to put outsiders on their backs pretty-smartish and much to the merriment of the locals.

My grandad Fred Aplin, was a traditional farmer and so are many of my family members who still 'till' the fields near the Blackdown Hills at Buckland St Mary. I still love to hear the stories from me ma Barbara, of the things that they used to get up to in that sleepy by-gone era which is fast disappearing,

Fred Aplin on the cider press

but there is much to be learnt about the old ways which shouldn't be dismissed. Especially their joy and sheer passion for harvesting apples from their local cider orchards and making sure that the cider was brewed and ready to be enjoyed and relished by the local community.

Much folklore has grown up around the making of cider where I am sure that our ancestors viewed it as something miraculous – its effects indeed often are! This, coupled with the old beliefs in spirits and various superstitions enabled the creation of some very unique customs which I am pleased to say are still being practiced today.

One of these is our traditional practice of 'Wassailing' where the people of the community gather together in the early part of the year to drink cider, make merry and look forward to a bumper harvest of cider apples ready to produce the next magical batch of cider. Incidentally the word Wassailing is Anglo-Saxon and means something like 'be in good health!' The response to the word 'Wassail' was always 'Drinc-Hael' which meant to 'drink and be healthy'!

In fact there is much more to this practice than meets the eye, and if you view this practice through the eyes of someone living and breathing our culture, and also working the land in olden times then it doesn't take much to picture how close our ancestors were to nature – they were almost part of the land that they toiled. Coupled with their beliefs in the spirits of nature, they would have indeed believed that it was good luck to appease them to ensure that nothing malevolent were to happen to the crops or the community.

Therefore the practice of Wassailing is a tradition that pacifies the spirits which may do harm to our beloved orchards, and during the ceremony the trees are given offerings of cider which is sprinkled on their bark and leaves while giving them blessings and protection. Some people may find this silly these days, but I have seen with my own eyes that others are keeping these traditions alive and have a deep reverence for them.

Modern cider production has somewhat blossomed into the huge industry which we are seeing today and the varieties of cider which are now on the market is beyond belief. Never has there been such a time when the people of Somerset have been blessed with so much choice for our regional brew, and I have seen many rosy cheeks because of it.

I can still remember me' pa Ray taking me out onto the Somerset levels to get his Scrumpy from a farmer that to my young eyes appeared to live in the middle of no-where, and who lived in a place that fascinated me, although it smelt a bit strange! I was only about 5 but I can still see the image of this strange man in big wellies, hay coming out of his coat pockets and the holes in his shirt, and the funny looking hat which he always had on his head.

His face was round and red just like an apple and his nose was the shape of a granny smith. 'Cum err me babber' he would say and would always let me have a sip of his golden homemade Scrumpy which I would always love, indeed I have never forgotten it.

It was from the people and characters like this, who loved and adored their cider that the big industries that we see today eventually emerged. Coming from small roots the love of cider has spread throughout the world, and we are now in an era where all can enjoy the benefits that come from drinking a lovely pint of the gold stuff (or orange depending on which variety you are drinking!).

Somerset is the 'number one' in cider making and always will be - testament to this statement is the amount of cider producers which are still thriving in the county. These days they not only make the still farm house 'scrumpy' cider that we all love, but there is now a huge variety of sparkling and still ciders with many varying flavours and strengths. Gone are the old-fashioned cider presses that the farmers would have sweated over to squeeze the delicious juice out of the apples, to be replaced with industrial sized cider presses which are now fully automated and which produce significantly more cider – oo'ar!

As you walk some of the trails in this book, please enjoy the variety of ciders which we are blessed with in this glorious part of the world, and if you are an outsider then remember to go easy – some are more potent than you might think… Either way, Enjoy!

The Aplin family - Haymaking during the early 20th Century
Near Buckland Saint Mary within The Blackdown Hills

The Queens Arms - Bleadon Village

Walk 1 - The Bleadon to Uphill Round Robin

This is a beautiful walk which is not too long and picks up from the start of the famous West Mendip Way trail. It is a pleasant section of the county with some fantastic views, a section of flat countryside, some lush green hills and a number of old pubs to whet your appetite with some

delicious Somerset Cider. This walk will also take you to the old and beautiful villages of Uphill by the sea and Bleadon which is inland, giving you the contrast of farming and nautical communities.

It will take you between 4 and 6 hours to complete this walk, depending on how long you spend in each Inn. If you are short of time or don't fancy walking for half the day then just walk one way, start at either village to turn this into a pleasing 3 hour stroll with refreshments!

(Distance: 6 miles)

Y ou will start your day in the beautiful Somerset village of Bleadon which nestles itself into the west end of the Mendip Hills. Bleadon is a stunning little settlement with a community that has been formed around farming for centuries. The

Pretty Cottages in the heart of Bleadon

village is surrounded with an array of cider orchards with some being used by a large and popular local producer.

People have been settled in the Bleadon area since at least the bronze age and a number of years ago the program 'Meet The Ancestors' dedicated a whole episode to this village. During the construction of some modern

The Church of St Peter and St Paul - Bleadon

houses at Whitegate Farm, the builders unearthed a skeleton that dates back over 2000 years and which they lovingly called 'The Bleadon Man'.

The archaeological team who investigated the find have come to the conclusion that he was most likely a farmer and that he was around 50 years old when he died – and undoubtedly The Bleadon Man would have loved a pint of cider to warm his cockles through those dark and cold winters in the bronze age. The team also DNA tested the population of Bleadon and remarkably there are four people living in the village that are related to this ancient figure. *We don't travel far in these parts!*

Make your way into the Queens Arms where you are going to start by having a nice cold pint of local cider. 'The Queens' as the locals call it has a selection of the modern drought ciders and also some still farmhouse ciders or 'scrumpy' as we like to call it round' eer!

The Queens Arms is a very old pub and is reputed to have been built in the 16th Century, just after the death of King Henry VIII of England. Ever since the local farmers have frequented this fine old pub which is oozing country charm and character, with open fires and old wooden beams throughout.

The beautiful Bleadon Village

After enjoying your first pint it is now time to get on the road – leave The Queens and turn right to head towards the centre of the village where you will get a glimpse of the stunning old church of St Peter and St Paul which was first being used back in 1317 AD.

Leaving the Queens and heading towards the village

However, before you get as far down the road as the church you will see Rectory Lane on your right which you are now going to head down. *Note: you are now on the West Mendip Way so you will also see their signs which will guide you along the path.*

Rectory Lane

Gate at the end of Rectory Lane

At the end of Rectory Lane you will see a small kissing-gate, pass through this and keep following the path. To your right you will be able to look across some beautiful green fields which further back, climb steeply to the top of Bleadon Hill.

Pass through another kissing-gate at the end of the lane and you will find yourself on a pretty section of road called Purn Way and which you will now follow to the west end of Bleadon Village.

Along the way you will pass by a sign post which is engraved with the words West Mendip Way and a string a quaint old Somerset cottages with beautiful gardens which are full of flowers and foliage.

Purn Way

Pretty bespoke cottages on Purn Way

Keep following Purn Way and towards the end of the road you will see a full size croquet lawn to your left. Straight in front of you will be the Bleadon Village Café which is a charming place with good service and lots of delicious food, and next to the café is the Village Stores which will be useful if you are in need to stock up your backpack! Purn Way passes in front of the café and before long you will find yourself at a T-junction where you will meet Bleadon Road. Look to your left here and take in the view across the fields which lie in front of this sleepy little village, in the distance you will see the majestic Brent Knoll hill. The area around Brent Knoll is completely flat so this hill really does make its presence known to all around.

Bleadon Croquet Lawn

Looking across the fields to Brent Knoll

Do Not step onto Bleadon Road, but instead look to your right where you will see a small wooden gate which is the entrance to the beautiful Purn Hill. Go through the gate and you will now be heading up the east side of the hill, to your left and on the other side of the wall is The Catherine's Inn which you may want go in for a pint - although I suggest you leave it until you come back to Bleadon later in the day.

20 Gate to Purn Hill   *Walk 1 - The Bleadon to Uphill Round Robin*

Half way up the side of Purn Hill you will find another gate and an information board which details some of the unique foliage and animal life which the area has to offer. After which you will turn right to follow the West Mendip Way along the side of the hill for about a quarter of a mile. This is

Looking back at Bleadon from the start of Purn Hill

a really nice section of path and it will lead you through an ancient woodland which is cool and moist.

Walking through Purn Hill Woods

To your right you will get the odd glimpse through the trees down to some of the village fields that sit below where you are now stood.

The path ascends gradually and near the top you will pass through two metal gates. Stop here and look back to your right – you will now get the most amazing vista with Bleadon Village in the foreground, the Somerset Levels in the middle and on a clear day the mystical Glastonbury Tor in the far distance which is about 16 miles away from here as the crow flies.

From here, the path goes back on itself and to the left of the gate which you have just passed through. Follow the wooded lane down the hill which will give you the occasional view across to The Quantock Hills which are some

Looking towards Glastonbury Tor from Purn Hill

View of the Quantock Hills from Purn Hill

10 miles away and also in the gorgeous Somerset countryside.

At the bottom of the hill you will emerge onto a small lane which is set back from the main A370 as it leaves the southern end of Weston-s-Mare. Turn right and make your way along this private little lane until you find yourself on the east side of the main road, which you will now have to cross. There can be fast moving traffic here to take your time and ensure that you cross here safely.

Once on the other side turn right and head towards Weston-s-Mare and Uphill. About 200metres along the road you will cross over the train track on 'Devils Bridge', but keep your eyes open because as soon as you cross the bridge you will need to turn left and back on yourself to follow a small and quiet lane which heads away from the A370. At the bottom of the lane there are a couple of houses and you will see a sign to direct you to the right and which keeps you on the West Mendip Way.

Quiet Lane adjacent to the A370

The view from Devils Bridge

Gate leading to a private road

Pass through a gate with the sign 'private road' mounted on it and you can now follow this pretty little path with lush green grass under-foot for the next half a mile.

From this lane you will be afforded with lovely views across to Brent Knoll to the south (on your left hand side) and about half way along you will start to get glimpses of the Old Windmill which has stood proudly up on top of Uphill Hill since the 18th Century (to your right hand-side). On the day that we passed through here the field to our left was full of young cows basking in the glorious sunshine.

Looking towards Brent Knoll with cows loving the sunshine

At the end of the lane you will go through a metal gate and turn right to head towards the stunning village of Uphill which is now only a stone's throw away. You will be walking on a cycle path which joins the sleepy village of Uphill to the holiday resort of Brean Sands which is a few miles away.

First glimpse of Uphill's Old Windmill

Looking north towards the Old Church of St Nicholas

Looking up from here you will get a beautiful view of the Old Church of St Nicholas which stands majestically on top of the hill. This path is a real gem and not only is it a pretty and pleasant section of the West Mendip Way, but as you approach Uphill you will also get some amazing views out across the Bristol Channel where you will often see boats and ships moving along its winding length. The view here is outstanding which has green foliage, Brean Down jutting out into the sea, the Bristol Channel, Welsh coastline and the Brecon Beacons in the far distance. You will also be able to see the islands of Steep Holm and Flat Holm which sit out in the middle of the channel.

The view to the Bristol Channel

The island of Flat Holm

The name 'Holm' comes from the Old Norse language which means island and it is interesting to note that the Vikings would use these islands as a base while attacking villages along the English Coastline.

Keep to the path and you will soon pass near Uphill Marina where there is an excellent café which serves some delicious food if you have the time to stop. Along this route you will see an old lime kiln and the remains of an old explosives store which used to be used in the early 20th century.

Once you get to the village turn right and follow the road towards The Dolphin Inn which is only a few minutes away.

Uphill's Old Lime Kiln

A pond and caravan park Near Uphill Marina

Along the left hand side of the road is a small river which you can often see ducks moving about on.

You are now in the beautiful seaside village of Uphill where Somerset's glorious River Axe meets the Bristol Channel. It is interesting to note that the source of the River Axe comes from Wookey Hole which is high up on the stunning Mendip Hill Range and has weaved its way for many miles back down to where you are now stood.

Uphill is very ancient and has been in use as a port since the Roman Empire, where it was believed to have been used to export lead which was mined up on the Mendips. It was also mentioned in the Anglo-Saxon

Uphill's little river where ducks are often seen

Domesday Book of 1086AD as *Opopille* which in Olde English meant *'above the creek'*. In fact our ancestors have lived in these parts for much longer, and during the industrious quarrying which was prevalent in Uphill during the 19th Century they discovered flint tools and animal bones which can be dated back 40,000 years! Apparently they also discovered a primitive cider press so our love of the apple in Zomerzet appears to be very old indeed!

'The Dolphin' public house - Uphill Village

There are a couple of really good pubs in Uphill *(The Dolphin and The Ship Inn)* and you will quench your first at the closest of these which is The Dolphin. It is also worth noting that you are also about 3 miles into today's walk and at the half way point, if this is enough for you then this is a good point to stop for the day and drink some glorious golden cider.

The main bar at 'The Dolphin'

En-route to 'The Ship Inn'

The Dolphin is a traditional village pub and is very popular with the locals, especially in the summer months when they often host some live music. It is an old pub which once burnt down back in 1860, but was soon rebuilt as I am sure that the locals wanted to get their cider haunt back up and running! Especially the local smugglers who would frequent this pub in times gone by.

The Dolphin has a selection of ciders to whet your appetite and a good selection of food, much of which is home cooked. The theme in the pub is all nautical, as you would expect from an old pub sitting next to the sea and is decked out with wooden beams and panelling.

Uphill Village - between The Dolphin and The Ship Inn

'The Ship Inn' - Uphill Village

After resting yourself and enjoying a lovely pint of cider, it is time to get moving and make your way to the next pub of the day. Luckily for you The Ship Inn is only about 60 seconds walk away – so don't panic, your next pint of cider is only minutes away!

The glorious Ship Inn has been a public house for over 250 years and in the past was frequented by smugglers and local reprobates – some things never change!! The Ship Inn is a lovely pub and its nautical theme is as strong today as it was nearly three centuries ago. It also has a good food menu, so like The Dolphin this is also a good place to take on board some food and cider.

Head towards the metal gate after leaving 'The Ship Inn'

Once you have enjoyed some good conversation with the locals and a delicious pint of cider then it is now time to get your walking legs on. Come out of the Ship Inn and head straight across the road to a narrow path which ascends towards an old small metal gate. Pass through the gate and you will now be heading up hill to the Church of St Nicholas which is perched on the summit.

Heading up the hill towards The Church of St Nicholas

Note: this path is quite steep and if you need a gentler route then come out of the Ship Inn, turn right and head to the end of the road where the Uphill Marina is located. Follow the path back the way you came - through the Marina and out into the fields beyond where the path will join up with the route which heads over the hill.

The view while ascending the hill towards the church

As you ascend up the side of the hill look back and you will get the most amazing views out over Uphill and all of the adjacent town of Weston-super-Mare. In the distance you will be able to see right across the Bristol Channel to the coastline of Wales on the other side. On a summers day this really is an amazing place to just sit and soak up the warmth whilst looking out across this part of Somerset.

Gate to the Church

Walk through the gate into the church graveyard and you will now be able to follow the path through the grounds to the gate which lies along its east wall. The old church of St Nicholas (or Old Nick as the locals call it) is very old and is actually the oldest building in the area which dates back to around the time of the Norman Conquest of 1066. However, legend has it that there may have been an even older Anglo-Saxon church on this site which dates back to the time of King Alfred the Great - King of the Anglo-Saxons from 886 to 899AD. The church doors are sometimes open, so if you have the time then it may be worth a peek inside.

The Old St Nicholas Church - or Old Nick!

The Old Windmill - Uphill

Once out of the church grounds you will be walking towards the remains of an 18th century Windmill. Go through the gate on the side of the windmill and the steps inside will lead you to its top where there is a viewing platform and information about what you are looking towards. The views from the top of here are stunning and you will be afforded with virtually 360° panoramic views.

To the south-east you will be able to look out over the Somerset levels and see Glastonbury tor which is 18 miles away. To the south you will see the beautiful and iconic Brent Knoll standing proud out of the flat land which lies below, behind which you will see the stunning Quantock Hills Range.

View South East - from The Old Windmill

View North West - from The Old Windmill

To the west you will look across Uphill Marina to Brean Down which juts out into the sea and to the north and north-west is Weston-super-Mare and views towards Wales across the Bristol Channel. This truly is a spectacular spot to enjoy the vista of this part of the gorgeous county of Somerset.

Leave the Old Windmill and walk south to slowly descend down the back of the hill with views down to the winding River Axe (Uphill Pill)

on its last stage before meeting the sea - you will most definitely see many boats which will be moored all along its length. At the bottom of the hill you will join with the path which comes from the Uphill Marina. In fact you are now back on the famous Mendip Way and at its starting point –

Looking down towards Uphill Pill - head towards the gate at the bottom of the hill

from here this long-distance trail makes its way right across the Mendip Hills to Frome which is 50 miles away and with an ascent of 6000ft (1828 metres). But don't worry, I can assure you that the walk back to Bleadon will be 'much' gentler!

Pass though the kissing-gate which you earlier came through and head out onto a path which will lead you towards the Bleadon Levels and the area of Walborough. You will be walking for a short time on the cycle path which was recently opened between Uphill and Brean and which makes for an easy section.

Go through the gate on the left - follow the lane back to the A370

After going through another gate you will shortly come across a path to your left. Go through the gate to enter the path which you earlier came along to Uphill from the A370 and which you will now follow for about a quarter of a mile.

Once back at the A370 cross over the road and head back down the quieter lane which you passed along earlier. From here you now have two options:

•   Either go back up Purn Hill which you came down earlier to take you over to Purn Way in Bleadon Village

•   Or follow the lane to its end.

If you decide to follow the lane to the end you will meet the A370 again where you can follow a short footpath around into the west side of Bleadon village. You will now pass by The Catherine's Inn which is decked out as a modern theme pub. However, this is another opportunity to have a nice pint of cider and some food.

Follow 'Bleadon Road' back to The Queens Arms

After The Catherine's Inn, follow Bleadon Road which will snake around the corner and go right into the heart of the village. You will get some beautiful views across the fields which lie in front of the stunning Bleadon village across once again to Brent Knoll.

Pretty cottages En-route to The Queens Arms

Follow the road for about a quarter of a mile which will take you past the village hall where the road bends to the left. Slightly up hill from here you will once again see the oasis of the Queens Arms which is your final destination for today, and where you can rest and of course – have another beautiful pint of cider... oo'ar!!

View across the fields before the Village Hall

Roger Wilkins - The Cider King!

Roger Wilkins with a pint of Scumpy

Roger Wilkins is one of, if not 'the last' of a fast-disappearing generation of cider makers, and is so passionate about his Scrumpy Cider that it is truly infectious. Just spending an hour or two around Roger is a real honour for many reasons. His hospitality is second to none, and as soon as I walked into his cider barn I was greeted with a friendly smile and asked instantly if I wanted a drink. A few more were to follow and I had one of the best mornings that I have had in a long time, chatting to Roger and some of his farm-hands & locals who were a really friendly bunch.

Traditional Spit and Sawdust

Now 71 years old (but you wouldn't guess it) Roger is still strong and 'fit as a fiddle' – which he puts down to his love of cider. In fact, he said that he hasn't ever seen a doctor or even taken a pain killer, which he puts down to drinking his beloved Scrumpy cider.

When asked about his cider I could clearly see a twinkle in his eye, before telling me a few stories of his love for the gold stuff. He has been drinking his family cider since the age of five, and says that it is 'purer than the water that comes from the tap', and I believe that he is right. There are no chemicals in any of his cider and he doesn't even add sugar to it, making his cider the purest and the most authentic that you can lay your hands on. It is delicious and very potent- well worth sampling.!

Some locals relaxing and enjoying a cider

Cheese and pickles are also on sale!

But if you are not used to drinking this type of cider then take heed as it could soon knock you off your feet!

Roger learnt the art of cider making from his grandad, where he was told to always mix the apples that he could lay his hands on from any of the surrounding orchards - which includes his families own old and beautiful orchard which stands proud on the hill behind his farm. Using no chemistry whatsoever, Roger was taught by his grandad how to produce his Scrumpy Cider from taste alone, and that is what he still does by checking how his cider tastes throughout every stage of its creation.

Over the years many people have gone to 'Land's End Farm' at Mudgley (near Wedmore) to sample his golden elixir, and this has included many famous people. If you get the time then ask Roger about some of the people that have flocked there over the years, it is indeed mind blowing as to who has been there to drink his Scrumpy.

All 'tasters' of his cider come in half pint measures and it is absolutely delicious, so once you have managed to find his farm – relax, sit back, enjoy some good conversation and savour the moment as you will be experiencing the Somerset cider culture at its finest.

It is no exaggeration to label Roger Wilkins as 'The Cider King' and long may he keep creating his amazingly scrumptious and intoxicating golden brew – I'm sure that there will be many sad cider drinkers in the area if he were to ever stop!

Wilkins Farmhouse Cider – Land's End Farm, Mudgley, Wedmore, BS28 4TU, Tel: 01934 712385

Walk 2 - The Mudgley to Godney Apple Cart Race

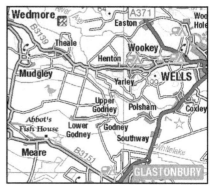

A beautiful walk which will guide you across the watery flat-lands of the Somerset Levels, to pick up two fantastic places to whet your first. One being the infamous Land's End Farm at Mudgley, where you will be able to sample the delights of real Scrumpy from Roger Wilkins. At the other end of the walk you will visit the pretty village of Godney and its vibrant pub 'The Sheppey'.

If 9 miles is too much for one day then just pick one of the cider houses to head towards and return to the car park – giving you a pleasing 4 mile stroll.

(Distance: 9 miles)

Y ou are going to start your day by making your way to the beautiful Somerset Levels at the car park to the stunning Westhay Moor Nature Reserve which is at the southern end of Dagg's Lane Drove. *Note: The nearest postcode is BA6 9TX which will take you to a house 1 mile to the west of the car park. Follow the road 'Westhay Moor Drove' to the east for about a mile and you will see the sign for the nature reserve and the adjacent car park.*

Lace up your boots and prepare yourself for a day that will bring quite an adventure and will enable you to experience the Somerset Cider Culture at its finest.

Westhay Nature Reserve Car Park

Head south to pass through the Westhay Nature Reserve entrance and walk to the end of the road which is directly in front of you. The road bends to the right here, so turn the corner and you will follow Westhay Moor Drove for about quarter of a mile.

Westhay Moor Drove, after leaving the car park

From the Drove you will get fine views across the Levels, and if you look behind you will see the majestic and mysterious Glastonbury Tor which is only a few miles from here.

The Somerset Levels cover an area of about 160,000 acres, and looking down from the Mendips they stretch out as far as the eye can see. The Levels have a long history and people have lived out on these watery marshes since at least 3800 BC, when the

Glastonbury Tor - from Westhay Moor Drove

whole area was flooded with water. Archaeologists have found ancient

wooden tracks preserved in the local peat bogs that the ancient inhabitants would use to get across the marshes.

Since before the time of the Domesday Book of 1086 the locals had already started draining the water from the Levels to uncover

Walking west on Westhay Moor Drove the land to be used for agriculture. These ancient farmers were also producing Scrumpy cider and this is also documented. In fact the first recordings of cider presses being used as a source of income in Somerset was in The Royal Charter of 1230.

Not much has changed and the local farmers are still producing and enjoying the delights of Scrumpy.

Once you get to London Drove (see photo) turn right and you will now enter the Nature Reserve where you can follow the track in a straight line for the next mile or so.

This is a very nice walk which will guide you between some pretty woodlands and will afford you glorious views across the wetlands which stretch out on either side. The wetlands are frequented by various migrating birds and you will see them all around on the water and

Turn right onto London Drove

in the hedgerows. There is also the occasional bird-hide which you can

Near the south end of London Drove

go in and take a rest while looking out on the beauty of the Somerset Levels. Behind this stunning setting you will also have the awe-inspiring backdrop of the Mendip Hill range.

Once at the end of London Drove you will now need to turn right to join the North Chine Drove. In front of you will be a view across a field to the small hamlet of Mudgley – in fact the farm which you can now see across the field is Land's End Farm and this will be your first point of call for the day to have a nice drink of cider.

Walk along the road for only a couple of hundred metres and on your left you will find a farm gate which will lead you into

Looking across the wetlands from London Drove

Land's End Farm - Cider Orchard Behind

this beautiful oasis of Scrumpy cider.

Look up above the farm and you will see the old apple orchard which the Wilkins family have been making their Scrumpy from since the mists of time.

On the gate post you will see a public footpath sign, so you will know you are going the right way. Follow the footpath across the field and this will lead you to this infamous cider house – Wilkins Cider at Land's End Farm.

Once inside you will be undoubtedly greeted by the owner Roger Wilkins or one of his friendly helpers, who will ask you if you would like a drink. There will only be the best traditional cider to drink here, so enjoy some time in Rogers Barn, have a delicious drink and maybe buy some of his amazingly tasty cheese.

The Gate to Scrumpy Heaven

It is so relaxing at Wilkins Cider that you may struggle to leave – but once you decide to get moving head back the way you came to the farm gate which is on the North Chine Drove.

Cider Trees in blossom

You are now going to turn left and make your way along this beautiful country lane for about a quarter of a mile. Keep your eyes peeled as you are now looking for the next track on your right.

Turn right onto Dagg's Lane Drove

This will once again be Dagg's Lane Drove which you can now walk along in a straight line for about a mile and a half.

You will be walking back across the Westhay Nature Reserve with stunning country views all around you.

The wetlands and lakes will once again be on either side of you which makes for a really pretty walk. At the southern end of this drove you will pass the car park on your left where you would have parked your car earlier on.

Depending on how you are doing regarding time, you may want to end your walk here for today – but on those lovely summer days with long daylight hours you may as well keep moving. Your next destination is going to be 2 miles away at the sleepy village of Godney and 'The Sheppey' for some food and drink.

Peaceful, pretty wetlands on The Levels

Pass by the car park and once again make your way to the entrance of the nature reserve. Once on the road you will now turn left to walk in an easterly direction on the 'Westhay Moor Drove'.

The views along here are really stunning with pretty hedgerows which surround lovely farmed fields, and to your

right you will be accompanied by the glorious vista of the mysterious Glastonbury Tor. Along the way you will also see a variety of different birds, there will be the odd cow in a field and to your left you will be accompanied along

Looking towards Priddy on The Mendips

the way by the spectacular view of the Mendips Hill Range.

On top of the Mendips you will be able to see a tall telecommunications mast which is adjacent to the desolate but beautiful village of Priddy – which you will see on one of the other walks in this book!

Just over a mile from the Westhay car park you will come to a crossroads where the road you are on will meet Tilleys Drove. Turn right here and head towards Godney and the fabulous 'Sheppey Inn' which is now only 1 mile away at Lower Godney – so don't panic, your next drink of delicious cider is not far away now!

Turn right onto Tilleys Drove

Approaching Lower Godney

At the end of Tilleys Drove there is a T-junction and you will need to turn left here – in fact you are now in Lower Godney, so nearly there!

Lower Godney is a beautiful hamlet that consists of just a few houses which line the road that you are now walking on. The houses here are all bespoke, as you would expect in the countryside and it is a very pretty place to enjoy a stroll – especially during the summer months.

Lower Godney

You will now arrive at The Sheppey which is an amazing pub that blends the traditional with the modern perfectly. Although it is an old building and has the look of a sleepy village pub, as soon as you walk through the door it is as if you have been transported to a different place entirely.

The Sheppey Inn

It is a very 'happening' pub and puts on events which include live bands and Dj's – much to the delight of the local residents of Somerset. However, you will still find peace and tranquillity here as they have got the balance between old and new just right.

Their menu is also excellent, so this is your chance to get yourself a really good meal before the next stage of today's walk.

First of all though, get yourself a glass from one of the barmaids and you will be able to fill it up yourself from a variety of Scrumpy ciders which they sell. Now it is time to relax, enjoy your cider and wait for your food to arrive – on a good day you will be able to do this is the pleasant surroundings of their beer/cider garden which runs adjacent to The Sheppey River at the back of the Inn, with

views out across the remaining Somerset Levels towards Glastonbury. The locals are also really great and I struck up a conversation at the bar with a man which had passed me in a car earlier that day after leaving Westhay - what a great bloke and he really helped me on that

afternoon, perhaps one day I will be able to repay the favour!

After you have had your fill of cider & food and the pleasant surroundings, it is now time to get moving again. You are now 2 miles away from the car park at Westhay Moor Nature Reserve so just enough distance to walk off your lunch.

To get back to the car park you are now going to take the same route which you followed earlier to get yourself to Lower Godney and which will take you between 45 mins and 1 hour, depending on how quick you are walking.

So, leave The Sheppey Inn and turn left to follow the road back to the corner where the road you are on meets Tilleys Drove. Turn right and after approximately a third of a mile you will be back at the crossroads where you will need to turn left onto Westhay Moor Drove.

Follow this drove for a mile and you will be back at the car park, and your final destination for this gorgeous day's walk. You will now be able to leave the Levels with a smile on your face and some fantastic memories of some of the characters which you would have met along the way – especially at Land's End Farm!

Wilkins Cider, Land's End Farm - Mudgley

The Stunning Glastonbury Tor

The Cider Barn

The Cider Barn is a unique live music and 'real cider' drinking venue which lies in the heart of Somerset – between the sleepy villages of Cheddar and Draycot. In fact, if you are visiting Cheddar for the day then you may as well top things off by a visit to 'The Cider Barn' as it is only a few minutes away by car.

The brainchild of Jason Law, it is without doubt one of the best places in the area to listen to some outstanding folk music, or relax to the hypnotic sound of the local artists during one of his many open-mic nights.

Upon meeting Jason it is obvious that this is a man who is completely passionate about what he is doing and loves the day-to-day running of his Cider Barn. He must be doing something right as he's happy and so are his many customers who love flocking to his venue to drink, listen to fine music and to also eat some of the excellent food which he has on offer. His staff are also very friendly and can be seen enjoying some conversation and smiles with the locals and passers-by.

There is a large selection of ciders available to drink, and you can also buy cider here to take away. Jason also stocks most of the Scrumpy ciders from the local producers, so if you are after a taste of 'real Somerset Scrumpy' - then pay him a visit and sample the local flavours! *The Cider Barn: A371, Latches Lane Crossroads, Draycott, Cheddar BS27 3RU. Tel: 01934 741837*

Walk 3 - The Priddy Cider Press Circular

A spectacular walk which will take you partly across the top of the vast Mendip Plateau. This is an old area where people have lived for 3000 years — you will get to see the evidence of this on top of North Hill where the ancient barrows (burial mounds) are located.

You will also take in the atmosphere of two old and beautiful Somerset Pubs, with some delicious cider to taste!

(Distance: 5.5 miles)

When you decide to embark on this walk, you are in for a real treat as you will be spending your day high up on The Mendips in the glorious area of Priddy. Priddy is the highest village in Somerset and lies on the large expanse of the Mendip Hills plateau with beautiful Somerset countryside all around it.

The Queen Victoria - Priddy

The start of your walk will be at The Queen Victoria which is just south of the village green on Pelting Drove and at a height of 1,000 feet above sea level. The pub started serving pints of cider and ale back in the late 1800's and is still going strong today. Once inside you will also see that it has also retained many of its original

The bar at The Queen Victoria

features with open fires, log burners, old wooden beams and an original flagstone floor.

This is a really great pub and the friendly staff will not only serve you some fine cider but the menu is also very popular, so this is a good place to

One of the rooms inside The Queen Victoria

have a nice meal before setting off – or at the end of today's walk.

Once leaving the Queen Victoria you will need to turn left and make your way towards the centre of the village and to the road junction which lies only a stone's throw away.

Looking left from here you will be able to see Priddy's large village green

Priddy Village Green

which stunning old houses lining its perimeter. In the middle of the green you will be able to see the Priddy Hurdle Stack, which are 'pens' that

were used to hold sheep during the village sheep fair. They are not used today but the sheep fair at Priddy is one that goes back many centuries.

Turn right at the junction and you will now head east towards The Hunters Lodge Inn which will be your second stop off on today's walk,

The Sheep Hurdle Stack on Priddy Green

for a nice drink of cider. The signpost here points towards Wells – so make sure that you walk in this direction.

You are now going to follow the road for the next 1.7 miles. This road is not too busy but keep your eyes open as

Turn right here and head onto the Wells Road

there can be fast moving traffic along this stretch. It is however a pretty walk and it will give you some fine views of the surrounding countryside and you will also pass by some stunning old Somerset houses.

En-route to The Hunters Lodge Inn

Just before The Hunters Lodge Inn you will pass by two large stones on either side of the road which mark the entrance to Priddy village before you reach a set of crossroads. You are now at your next destination as to your right you will see the impressive structure of the inn.

The Hunters Lodge Inn is a fantastic old pub that has been under the same management for many decades. The interior is very traditional, with big open fireplaces and beautiful old wood panelling. There is an excellent

The Hunters Lodge Inn - Priddy

selection of ciders and ales on sale here so I can vouch that you will not be disappointed, and will now be able to quench your first after the first part of today's walk. There is also a

good selection of home-cooked food available here so this is another good opportunity to sit down, relax and enjoy a nice meal.

Once you have had your fill and are ready to leave you will need to come out of The Hunters Lodge and turn left to head back on the road which you walked along earlier from The Queen Victoria.

Keep your eyes open for a public footpath which will be on your right after half a mile, there is a signpost on the left hand side of the road to help guide you (pointing across the road).

Follow the public footpath on a lane which passes a house on the left and which has a pretty wooded area to the right - you are now walking on The Monarchs Way.

Before long you will see 'The Belfry' which is the base to one of the Priddy

Turn right to join The Monarchs Way

Caving Clubs and which has some well-placed benches to the front of the building. So an opportunity to stop and have a quick break before moving on.

At the back of the Belfry's garden there is a stile which you will need to step over, after which you will cross over the adjacent lane to then pass through a small gap in a wall to walk out onto a track.

The Belfry - one of Priddy's Caving Clubs

Note: You will now follow this track all the way over the hill to nine barrows lane which lies about 1.5 miles away.

At the start of this track you will be weaving through a nice, cool woodland which is quiet and very serene. Along this route I could also see patches of bluebells which littered the low lying grasses on either side of the path.

Leaving The Belfry on The Monarchs Way

Follow The Woodland Track En-Route to Fair Lady Well

After approximately half a mile you will come across Fair Lady Well which is an ancient holy well and a place of reverence for local people going back to the prehistoric period. This is a very special place and it is well worth sitting quietly here for a few minutes and taking in the atmosphere.

Fair Lady Well

It is also worth noting that the surrounding area was once mined by the Romans who occupied the Mendips to mine lead, this was then sent back to Rome to be used in their plumbing and drainage networks.

Turn left and ascend after Fair Lady Well

Leaving Fair Lady Well you will need to take a sharp left to head up North Hill which stands at a height of 307m.

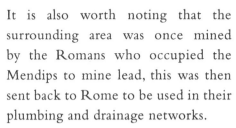
Looking back as you ascend North Hill

This is a really beautiful section of this walk and you will now be out in the glorious Somerset countryside with fields all around you and spectacular views of the surrounding low lying land. As you ascend, look back and you will be able to see the Stockhill forest which consists mainly of pines – and beyond that the ever present telecommunications mast which stands proud on the outskirts of Priddy.

To your left there will also be a drystone wall which you will follow all the way to the top of North hill – so if you don't see this wall you are probably heading in the wrong direction!

The view over the drystone wall to your left

Along this wall you will see some old Hawthorn trees which line the way at various points, and near the top of the hill you will see a round concrete water tank.

An Old Hawthorn with May Blossom

Once on top of North Hill look to your left as you will almost be in touching distance of some ancient barrows. North Hill at Priddy is littered with these 3000 year old burial chambers and this is testament to how long people have been living in this area. In fact there are also the

Ancient 'Barrows' on your left

remains of large 'Henges' at Priddy, and they must have been amazing to behold as Stonehenge is much smaller in comparison. In front of you will be a fence and a gate which you can pass through into the next field where the famous Nine Barrows are located.

As soon as you walk into this field there will be two barrows directly in front of you, and looking right across the other side of the field you will see a row of nine barrows which dominate the landscape – this really is something to behold.

Pass through the gate at the top of North Hill

Looking across North Hill to the Barrows

The Amazing Nine Barrows at Priddy

You can now either walk across to the nine barrows or just walk straight down the hill by following the drystone wall which is to your left.

Head downhill towards the gate at the bottom

At the bottom of the hill you will see a kissing-gate which you will need to pass through to move onto 'Nine Barrows Lane'. Turn left and you will follow Nine Barrows Lane back towards Priddy Village.

The gate leading to Nine Barrows Lane

I really loved this section of the walk as it is very quiet and picturesque here. The lane is lined on either side by old drystone walls, ancient trees, damp ferns, mosses, and you will also pass by Priddy Pool which will be about half a mile along the lane and on the right.

On Nine Barrows Lane - towards Priddy Village

Ferns and mosses on Nine Barrows Lane

Depending on what time of year you are doing this walk, you will either see the pool full of water or on occasions it will be completely dry – especially after a long hot spell in the summer months.

Priddy Pool

Stay on Nine Barrows Lane and shortly you will see a public footpath sign which leads you to the left, between some houses. You are now back on the outskirts of Priddy Village.

Pass between the houses on a track to find a gate, which leads onto a field

Turn left here, near some houses

which is a public right of way. Cross this small field to pass through another gate which will now guide you to the Church of St Lawrence.

This church is very old and records show that it was constructed in the 13th century, and it is also a Grade 1 listed building. This is a very beautiful place and the benches in the

Head for the gate at the end of the lane

churchyard make for an excellent spot to stop and take a well-deserved break. If you have the time then a look around the inside of the church is well worth doing, especially to see some of the 15th century carpentry which the interior boasts.

On the other side of the churchyard there are two gates - you will need to pass through the gate which is on the right where you will see another gate just behind it. Go through

First glimpse of Priddy's Old Church

both gates and turn right to walk just up the road, here you see a lane branching off to the left. Follow this lane downhill and you will soon be back on the main road, coming into Priddy Village from the north.

The Church of St. Lawrence

Turn left and follow this road back to the heart of the village, and shortly you will once again see the vast village green – on the other side of here is The Queen Victoria and the end of this fantastic walk.

Turn left, descending towards the heart of Priddy

Turn left and head towards Priddy village green

Back in the heart of Priddy village

It is now time to put your feet up and relax with a lovely pint of Somerset cider - you will be able to enjoy the comfort of your surroundings while thinking back over the fantastic memories which you would have created, while spending some time at the ancient and picturesque village of Priddy.

Put your feet up and have a cider in The Queen Victoria Inn

My Grandad Fred Aplin (right) with Ken Osmond on the cider press -
At Rolstone Court Farm, Hewish, Somerset (circa 1950's)

Thatchers - Somerset Cider at its Heart

Thatchers Cider is without doubt one of the UK's most loved cider producers and really doesn't need much of an introduction. Coming from humble roots in the beautiful county of Somerset, this company has now spread their delicious cider varieties across the globe - allowing our traditional, local pint to be tasted and enjoyed by thousands.

They are a traditional, family-run business whose story starts way back in

1904, when William John Thatcher made his first farmhouse cider at Myrtle Farm, and much to the delight of the local farm workers.

Over a hundred years later and Thatchers now have a fantastic range of ciders to satisfy every type of taste bud and cider connoisseur. With a variety of flavours and strengths, they really have taken cider producing to a whole new level.

The family are keen to grow a wide variety of cider apples, and as you travel through the Somerset countryside you will be able to spot some of their large and beautiful apple orchards – if you know where to look that is! They are a sight to behold, especially in late summer when you start to see the delicious cider apples in all of their glory.

It is an exciting time for us locals, as we know that they will soon be pressed - to extract their delicious juices for the next batch of Thatchers amazing cider.

If you are visiting the county, then make sure that you find yourself some time to head over to Myrtle Farm where the Thatchers Mill still is. It is a great place to visit, relax and try some of their ciders.

On site there is also a Cider Shop where you can try some tasters before buying, a cider house and restaurant called 'The Railway Inn' and if you have more time on your hands then I highly recommend the Thatchers tour which is a very informative and enjoyable way to spend the afternoon.

The Railway Inn is a wonderful place to stop for the day and have some fine food and a delicious pint of Thatchers cider. It is the Thatcher family's own pub, and I can assure you that you won't be disappointed as the surroundings are stunning - with open fires, beautiful leather chairs to relax on and one of the nicest looking, bespoke wooden bars that you could lay your eyes on.

So after going for one of the walks in this book, why not make your way to Sandford, put your feet up and enjoy a nice cold pint of Thatchers delicious cider.

Thatchers Cider

Myrtle Farm, Station Rd,

Sandford, Winscombe BS25 5RA

Tel: 01934 822862

Walk 4 - The Minehead to Porlock Apple Taster

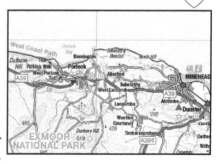

This walk provides a beautiful start to the day, which will give you some fine views over Exmoor and also across the sea to the Welsh coastline.

There are two official routes once on top of Exmoor; one route is inland and crosses Exmoor with limited views of the sea, whilst the other 'rugged-route' winds its way up and down the cliffs adjacent to the Bristol Channel. The rugged-route is by far the harder of the two walks, but you will be rewarded with some beautiful coastal scenery. This is also the first section of The South West Coast Path - so lace up your boots and enjoy!

You will need to get transport back to Minehead at the end of this walk, so make sure that you enquire about bus routes or taxi numbers before setting off! (Distance: 9.5miles / Ascent: 556metres)

Y ou will start your day at the fabulous pub, 'The Old Ship Aground' in the very scenic setting of Minehead Harbour. This is a very popular pub and testament to this statement is the amount of locals that love drinking here. The menu is also

The Old Ship Aground - Minehead Harbour

excellent, so this will be a great place to end your day, have a hearty meal and some delicious cider after your long day's walk over part of Exmoor.

Walking through the woods up North Hill

The start of this walk is a pleasant one and 'breaks you in gently' as you begin on a nice gradual flat section. From Minehead Harbour the path takes you between the slopes of a hill on your left which is covered in foliage and views out to the sea on your right before the path ascends steeply up the side of North Hill.

Along this short section you will see a row of quaint, old fisherman's cottages and you can also take in the view of some fishermen's boats which will be moored in the harbour.

A glimpse of the sea from the woods

Savour the view as you are soon going to enter an old woodland with a steep climb up the side of North Hill.

Leaving the last signs of civilisation behind for the day the path now ascends steeply and in a zig-zag fashion to get you to the top of the hill.

It's a fairly tough but pleasant hill to climb and until you get to the top you will be walking in an old but beautiful woodland. I really enjoyed this small section and the surroundings more than make up for the lack of sea views. As you get higher you will be walking in the woods on a fairly level track which will go through the National Trust area of Greenaleigh Point - you will also pass by a farm with the same name.

Eventually you will emerge from the woodland where your view will open up at the top of North Hill (250m, 820ft). You are now on top of Exmoor near a small car-park and the views are

Near the top looking down at the coastline

indeed spectacular. You will be able to see the rolling hills of Exmoor disappearing to the West and if you look to the North on a clear day you will see Wales on the other side of the Bristol Channel.

Not too far along the path you are presented with two separate and official routes which you can now take. One of these takes you across the top of the Exmoor hills while the other option (the alternative rugged route) will send you up and down along the edge of the hills which descend towards the sea.

I stopped for a quick chat with an elderly local lady which I had just bumped into, and after taking her advice I opted for the rugged route. She said it was a pleasant section to walk and recommended it to me before setting off on her way along the easier top route. *Note: both routes are sign-posted, so it is fairly easy to find your way.*

Foxgloves all along the path

Looking back she must have found it most amusing as she had sent me on the path that ascends and descends for much of the way, and due to the time of year the path was often obscured by ferns which grew in droves on either side. Having said that it was a very enjoyable section to walk with amazing views out to the sea and with the added bonus of not seeing another soul for some miles.

Note: the rugged path will add to the distance and about an hour to your walk.

Looking back towards Minehead

Dramatic Coastal Scenery

I now noticed for the first time that the sea was starting to turn a deep blue colour, as up to that point the Bristol Channel is subjected to huge tidal ranges which churn up the silt and mud from the seabed to give it the look of mud-soup. The Bristol Channel has one of the largest tidal ranges in the world, with the

The rugged route has some fantastic coastal scenery

A much needed break

height difference between the high and low tides being as much as 15 metres.

From this point onwards the sea water all around the Coast Path turns clear and blue which gives rise to some of the most beautiful scenery that I have ever had the pleasure to see. Due to the time of year the carpet of lush green ferns all around me was also broken up by dots of tall pink foxgloves. Foxgloves grow wild along most sections of the coast path during the summer months which really adds to its beauty.

Incidentally, I have now walked both of the paths on this section of the coast (the inland route at a later date) and both are very pleasant walks, although the higher inland path does not have the sea views that the rugged route affords you.

On the Rugged Route from North Hill to Hurlstone Point

The alternative rugged route re-joins the inland official route just before Hurlstone Point where you are still up high on the hills of Exmoor. I sat here for some time and took in the wonderful view which spread out before me.

I will never forget my first walk on this section of the coast path, and as the summer's sun still warmed me I took in my surroundings while having some refreshments.

The view here was inspiring as I could see the Welsh coastline in the distance, the rolling hills of Exmoor, and below me the flat beach which sits in front of the sleepy village of Porlock, which is also surrounded by the backdrop of Exmoor. The view of the sea sits in amongst all of this, and as I looked down I watched the sun shimmering upon its surface on this calm, warm day.

Looking towards Porlock Bay

Looking out into the distance you will also be able to admire the beautiful but jagged coastline of West Somerset as it disappears off towards North Devon. The inlets and headlands go as far as the eye can see and this view is just stunning.

The impressive Porlock Bay from Hurlstone Point

From here the path now takes you one of two ways, you can either drop down to the beach and walk along it to Porlock or alternatively you can make your way down the hill to Bossington via 'Allerford Woods', which on this occasion I opted to do *(Note - I have now taken both routes and preferred the woodland option).*

The walk down through Allerford woods was pleasant and not too steep and in places the sun was breaking through the leaves of the woodland canopy to shine down in patches on the floor around me.

At the bottom of the hill I crossed a small stream via an attractive old foot bridge before stopping on a well-placed bench for a quick cup of tea. I was now ready to begin moving on again for the last section of the day. As you will be finishing your walk at Porlock, you will now make your way through the stunning hamlet of Bossington.

What a treat is install for you here as Bossington turned out to be one of the most beautiful villages that I have ever seen.

The architecture of the old houses and cottages is just astounding with many of the dwellings having very beautiful, thatched roofs.

Approaching Bossington

After leaving Bossington, you will now make your way along the road into Porlock which isn't too far away.

You will head down-hill while following the main road to Porlock and before long you will start to see the first signs of this stunning little Somerset village.

Beautiful Bossington

Kitnors Tea Room Bossington

Make your way along the high-street and very soon you will come across The Royal Oak Inn which will be on your right. Here you will be able to have a nice cold pint of cider and some delicious food.

If you are planning on staying then this is a good village to spend the night, recharge your batteries and of course drink some more delicious cider.

The next walk in this book will take you on a circular route around Porlock Weir (which is a mile up the road) - so maybe you can stay the night in Porlock and turn this into a two day break with some good walks, delicious food and golden cider.

The Royal Oak Inn is a highly rated pub by locals and visitors which has excellent food, great service and a relaxing atmosphere. So make sure that you give yourself enough time so sit back and enjoy this part of Somerset.

Rich's Farmhouse Cider

L ocated out on the Somerset Levels in Watchfield, you will find Rich's Cider which is one of the best cider producers in the area. After you park your car and step out you will be confronted with one of their beautiful cider orchards, where you can often see sheep lying around in the shade coming from the leaves and branches.

Started by Gordon Rich at Mill Farm back in 1954 the business has grown from strength to strength – but the method of cider production has pretty much stayed the same, with their superb farmhouse cider being a very popular drink in the area.

In their farm shop you will also be able to pick up a variety of foods and cider making memorabilia. It has a lovely aroma of cider in the air - so when you walk through the door, breathe deep and take in the real smell of Somerset cider apples.

Once you have spent some time in their cider shop and have tasted some of their delicious ciders, it would be a good idea to make your way into their on-site restaurant where there is a wide variety of home cooked, traditional food.

They also have a cider museum which is well worth a visit, where you will be able to see some of the old machinery that was used to produce our local brew.

So if you are on the south-west side of the Mendips near Highbridge, make your way across to Rich's and pick yourself up some fine Scrumpy cider.

Rich's Cider Farm, Watchfield,

Highbridge, Somerset, TA9 4RD

Tel: 01278 783651

Above - Bleadon Cider Orhards

An Old Cider Orchard on the Somerset Levels near Burtle

Walk 5 - The Porlock Weir Knee Trembler

This is a beautiful walk across part of the spectacular Exmoor National Park. It is also a very quiet section, so make sure that you come prepared with all supplies that you will need for the day.

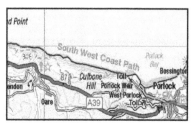

However, you will visit two fantastic places for a pint of cider - which will quench your thirst after this hilly walk. (Distance: 5.5 miles)

Y ou are going to start your day at the sleepy hamlet of Porlock Weir where you will find two pubs, a car park and a small harbour with boats bobbing up and down in the water. If you look back from here you will get a clear view of Hurlstone Point *(from Walk 4)* rising majestically on the opposite side of Porlock Bay.

The Anchor Hotel

Make your way into The Anchor Hotel which is a friendly establishment, and where you will be able to purchase a lovely drink of cider to whet your thirst before setting off on this fantastic walk. The Anchor Hotel is an amazing place, and once inside you will be able to take in it's quirky surroundings and decor. It has wood panelling throughout the building and many ornaments, carvings and statues will surround you. This really is a very attractive place to start your day and I can assure you that you won't forget it.

Porlock Weir Harbour and The Anchor Hotel

The Ship Inn is next door to The Anchor - and this is where you will end your walk later on!

The path now leads you down an alleyway between the Ship Inn & the Anchor Hotel, and you will now be heading to the tiny settlement of Culbone with its famous and ancient church. In fact you will also be on

The National Trail Acorn symbol on a tree.

The South West Coast Path, so for now just follow the small signs with 'acorns' on them, which is the National Trail symbol.

After leaving the alleyway you will find yourself on a section of path which takes you through pretty woodlands and also skirts along the bottom of a couple of fields – both of which give you glimpses out to the blue sea. On this occasion, upon going through a 'kissing-gate' to enter one of the fields I was confronted with a herd of sheep who, much to my amusement, were either lying in the sunshine or attempting to lie in the shadows of the bushes at the bottom of the field. They soon got out of my way though, and they looked surprised to see me appear and disturb their tranquillity.

Just after the field I stopped at an area that gave me a view out to the shimmering blue sea, which looked amazing in the summer sunshine. It was a rather pleasant spot to take a break, with lush green fields below me and with the stunning blue sea behind them. Behind me was an old wall with dozens of ferns and a ring of pink foxgloves growing out of and around it. The peace and quiet here was pleasantly broken by the occasional buzz of a honey bee drifting by.

In the ancient and beautiful Yearnor Woods

After my quick break I put my 'best foot forwards' and the path eventually led me up on to Worthy Toll Road which is an attractive lane with lush bushes on either side.

Worthy Combe Toll House

A treat awaits you at the end of Worthy Toll Road as you will be confronted by Worthy Combe Toll House which is one of the prettiest and unusual thatched houses that you could ever lay your eyes on.

Pass through the gate on the right-hand side of the toll house and head once again towards the hamlet of Culbone. On the side of the house is a small notice board which gives the service times for the tiny Culbone Church which you are heading towards. The path you are now walking on is the way that local parishioners have got themselves to church in all weathers for hundreds of years.

A stone seat built into a wall – Yearnor Woods

The path will take you through the enchanting Yearnor woods within which you will come across the remains of an old but significant dwelling. The odd limestone wall can be seen in amongst the ferns and moss which gives it an appealing character, which also has a lot charm.

It just shows us how nature can reclaim land which people have finished with, and it is quite profound to see the woods taking back what was theirs.

On this section of the path you will also pass through the 'fairy tunnels' which I believe were once linked to the ruins of the old building.

The Fairy Tunnels in the ancient Yearnor Woods

After a fairly lengthy but pretty walk you will eventually come across the hamlet of Culbone which consists of a few houses and the pretty Culbone Church - which claims to be the smallest church in England that is still in use, and dedicated to the Welsh Saint Beuno. It is as if you have stumbled across an oasis, as Culbone is a small clearing which is surrounded by dense woodland on all sides.

If you have the time I recommend that you take a look inside as it is a real gem. The church door is often left open and they encourage visitors to go inside. Culbone church is very old and testament to this is the fact that it was recorded in the Domesday Book (1086AD). Seating around 30 people during services it is indeed a tiny church, but was big enough

to meet the needs of the local community. In fact it still is big enough as there are only a few houses in Culbone and the population here is still very small, which consists of only 9 people. If you take a walk through the small cemetery which surrounds the church you will see the surname 'Red' engraved on to many of the gravestones – the Reds

The Picturesque Culbone Church

must have been a very influential family in the area as there appears to be many generations of them buried here.

There are a number of benches along the side of the cemetery which are next to an old limestone wall. I decided to sit here for a while and bask in the summer sunshine while taking the opportunity to have some lunch from my supplies, it was a very pleasant place to sit on that summer's day and it is an excellent spot to break up your days walk.

Incidentally, it is reputed that the famous poet Samuel Taylor Coleridge lived in Culbone at Ash Farm for a while back in the late 18th Century, and it was during his time here that he got much of his inspiration for one of his most famous and opium induced poems 'Kubla Khan'.

Inside the tiny Culbone Church

Leaving Culbone you now progress on a section of the path which winds its way through the very ancient Culbone Woods. Culbone Woods are termed an 'Atlantic Oakwood' which are often described as Britain's temperate

Memorial to Sir David Calcutt adjacent to the benches

rainforest. The clean, moist coastal air results in lush vegetation - from trees and shrubs, to ferns, mosses and lichens, all can be seen to thrive in this damp micro-climate.

A waterfall in the ancient Culbone Woods

The woods can often feel slightly eerie which is not surprising as they have quite a history - they are believed to have been inhabited by people since at least 3500BC. In more recent times the woods were also used to banish the undesirables in society

A glimpse of the sea from Culbone Woods

which included criminals and those labelled as 'witches'. I say eerie, as the first time that I walked through these woods I could of literally have heard a pin drop, it was the middle of the day but as I stood still I could hear nothing, not even the sound of a bird or even the wind blowing through the branches and leaves on the trees.

During the 16th century the woods were also used to banish people from society who had contracted leprosy, and it is interesting to note that a leper colony was in use here for many years, with the unfortunate people having to live in makeshift homes which were dotted throughout the woodland.

After a short section of path you will come across a junction where the South West Coast Path can take you in two different directions (both are official routes). Here you will need to take the left hand path which will point you towards Silcombe Farm where there is also a B&B. *Note: if you were to keep walking west along The South West Coast Path you would soon be in North Devon which is now only a few miles away!*

Finger-posts showing the way to Silcombe Farm

Devon coat of Arms

Withy Combe, En-route to Silcombe Farm

Moving on, you will now have a pleasant walk up through the woods of Withy Combe which is a very pretty section.

At the top of the Withy Combe track

Looking across to Porlock Bay

The idyllic setting of The Parsonage

At the top of the path you will arrive at Silcombe Farm where you will now have to turn left to walk along Yearnor Mill lane - which will pass by The Parsonage, Ash Farm (where Samuel Coleridge lived) and Yearner Farm. The views along Yearnor Mill Lane are incredible as you will be at a height of approximately 300m with low lying land towards the sea. Looking down from here you will be able to see the blue ocean over the top of Culbone Woods, and some attractive fields which often have sheep on them. In fact, you can pretty much see the whole of Porlock Bay with the rolling hills of Exmoor lying behind it.

Looking back at the stunning Parsonage

Follow Yearnor Mill Lane until you get to a junction at Yearnor Mill Bridge, turn left here to head downhill towards Worthy once again (where you saw Worthy Toll House earlier).

Ash Farm - where Samuel Coleridge once lived for a while

You are now on the aptly named Worthy Toll Road, which is a nice walk through an old woodland (Worthy Woods) on a fairly sturdy track. The descent can be quite steep along this road, and you will be glad that you're walking downhill instead of ascending!

Worthy Toll Road

At the bottom of the hill you will be back at a junction with the South West Coast Path, turn right here and head back towards Porlock Weir – this is the path which you started your walk on and it will lead you back to The Ship Inn for some delicious food and a cold pint of the gold stuff.

Steep descent on Worthy Toll Road

Porlock Weir is very old and it is said that the harbour was built at around 1422AD. Smuggling in Somerset and especially at Porlock was rife in times gone by and during the reign of King Charles II the surveyor-general for customs was sent to Somerset to write a report. He was horrified by what he uncovered, and he mentions that every small port in Somerset was full of corruption and that smuggling was active at all of them! I bet we didn't serve him up any of our precious cider which I am sure was kept hidden away.

Head into The Ship Inn and it will now be time to put your feet up and

The beautiful Ship Inn – Porlock Weir

enjoy its unique atmosphere. This is one of the oldest inns in the county and it was built way back in 1290, although there was reputedly another inn on the same ground before this date.

Folk music has always been a tradition at The Ship Inn, and this tradition is still going strong today as the owners like to hold the occasional folk festival – so if you are lucky enough you will be able to enjoy some fine music to accompany your cider on your visit here.

An Apple Orchard on the edge of the Mendips

Hecks Farmhouse Cider

The Hecks family have been making traditional farmhouse cider in Somerset for almost two centuries. In fact the secret to this family's cider passion has been passed down through six generations, making them one of the longest standing cider producers in the area.

Their success started back in 1841 when their ancestors would make their delicious cider for their own use, and for the hard working farm labourers who would always enjoy some bread & cheese and a nice pint of cider after a long days toil on the fields.

The Hecks family's passion for their cider is infectious, and from the minute you walk through the door to their amazing farm shop you will be greeted with a smile from one of the family members – who will then guide you through their large variety of Scrumpy ciders with some gorgeous tasters.

They have a mind-boggling 24 different varieties of Scrumpy available, so you will definitely not be disappointed after a trip to their farm shop – and will be sure to come away with some of their golden nectar.

All of their cider comes from their locally grown and old apple orchards which the family are very proud of, in fact one of their orchards sits under the beautiful setting of Glastonbury Tor. It is therefore no surprise that you can taste the beautiful surroundings in their cider, which is absolutely delicious. Their cider is  also fermented in old wooden barrels which really adds to its flavour, giving it an old and rich taste. Once on your tongue your taste buds will transport you back in time, as the cider making techniques which they use haven't changed for centuries – so you will really be tasting what our local ancestors would have enjoyed and a part of Somerset history.

 The farm shop at Hecks Cider has been in use since 1896 and at one time was a traditional cider barn where the locals would meet to relax, drink cider and enjoy some good company. Today you will also be able to enjoy the barn, where they also sell a large variety of other farm produce, which include various cheeses, vegetables and the other drinks which they also produce on site – including apple juice and their gorgeous Perry which is fermented from their own pear orchards.

So, if you're in the Glastonbury area make sure that you head over to Hecks Cider and taste their 'real' Somerset Cider.

Hecks Farmhouse Cider, 9-11 Middle Leigh, Street
Somerset, BA16 0LB, Tel: 01458 442367

Walk 6 - The East to West Harptree Full Flagon

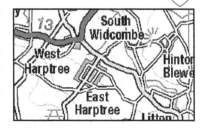

This is an easy walk on some fairly flat terrain – making it a very pleasant stroll on a sunny afternoon. You will be able to spend some time in the beautiful villages of East and West Harptree, which are tucked into the north side of the Mendip Hills.

More importantly, you will also be able to visit some fantastic pubs on this pleasant walk – allowing you the time to have some excellent cider and a plate of home-cooked food, enjoy!

(Distance: 3 miles)

Y ou are going to start the day in the stunning old village of East Harptree, which is sandwiched between the beautiful Mendip Hills and overlooking the view of Chew Valley, which lies to the north of the village.

The Waldegrave Arms

Your first point of call for today is going to be at The Waldegrave Arms which is located right in the heart of the village. This is a great pub which is decked out with its original old beams, log burners and with a feel of old Somerset.

After enjoying a lovely pint of cider, make your way out of the front door and turn left to head towards the picturesque village church which is dedicated to St. Lawrence.

The Church of St Lawrence - East Harptree

East Harptree

You will be amazed by your surroundings as this really is a very beautiful area and quintessentially English to the core.

To the right of the church gate you will see an old stone stile which is placed in the church wall with some steps leading up to it. Pass through this stile and you will now be able to follow a path which circumnavigates its way around the church boundary. You are now on your way to the nearby village of West Harptree.

At the end of the path you will be at another stone stile which you will pass through to enter a field that lies to the rear of the church.

Stone Stile in the church wall

Walk across the field which will give you some beautiful views out across the Chew Valley, you will also be able to see Chew Valley Lake in the distance. The lake is a huge reservoir and is in fact the 5th largest man-made lake in the United Kingdom with an area of 1200 square acres, and supplying much of the drinking water to Bristol.

The view across to Chew Valley Lake

Follow this lane after crossing the field

On the other side of the field, pass through a farm gate and you will find yourself on a pleasant grassy lane with lush green hedges on either side and which will keep you descending gently.

Towards the end of this lane you will walk through a small wooded area which is surrounded with old oak trees, giving you some cool shade on a sunny day. This is a good spot to stop for a break and just soak up the atmosphere for a while.

Wooded area with old Oak Trees

Moving on you will have to cross another stone stile before entering a field which you will now cross by following a path straight through its centre. On the day that I passed through here I was surrounded by lush, green wheat which was swaying in unison to a gentle breeze.

Follow the path across the field

There are other paths which lead away from the one that you are on, but for this walk stay in a straight line until you reach a small gate in a hedge at the fields other side (see pic below).

Pass through the gate and you will now be on a section of path with a farm on your right hand side, with some tall trees towering above a fence.

You will go through two more gates in short succession before finding yourself on a small field with a children's play-park at the end of it. You are now on the outskirts of West Harptree and won't be far from your next destination for today.

Go through this gate

First signs of West Harptree - cross to the lane by the white house

Cross the field and keep the hedge to your left, and at the other side you will enter a lane between a house and a tall wall.

The church of St. Lawrence - West Harptree

Follow the lane to its end and you will now be on the main road which passes through West Harptree and at the centre of the village.

Look to your left and you will now be able to see the glorious site of the church which dominates the view in the centre of the village, and is a very pretty spectacle. Being built in the 12th century, the church of St Mary's is still much in use today and is a focal point for the local community.

Just in front of the church you will now be able to spot The Crown Inn which also lies at the centre of this affluent little village. This is your next destination for today and you will be pleased to hear that it is now time to quench your first with a cool pint of cider.

The Crown Inn - West Harptree

You will find a good variety of ciders at The Crown and an excellent food menu – so this is a good point in today's walk to also stock up on some calories! On a sunny day, make sure that you head round to the back of the pub and enjoy your cider and food in the beautiful setting of their beer (cider) garden.

Once you have decided to get moving again and continue your walk in the stunning Somerset countryside, you will now be presented with two options:

1.   Carry on with the walk which will now take you straight back to East Harptree.

2.   Take a diversion to pick up another pub in West Harptree – The Blue Bowl Inn.

If you have time on your hands and fancy picking up the second pub in West Harptree, then upon leaving The Crown Inn you will need to turn right and head down the road which is signposted towards Chew Valley Lake and which lies between the church and the pub.

Follow this road if you are going to
The Blue Bowl Inn

Note: Going to The Blue Bowl Inn will add a few miles and possibly another couple of hours to your days walk.

You will find The Blue Bowl Inn on the right hand side of the road if you opt to extend today's walk. After leaving 'The Blue Bowl' you will need to go back along the road which you took to get to the pub, and walk back to The Crown Inn before picking up the rest of today's walk.

The Blue Bowl Inn - West Harptree

The main road through West Harptree

Back at, or upon leaving The Crown Inn you will need to turn left and follow the main road back through the centre of West Harptree. Shortly you will be at a left bend in the road, at this point you will need to look straight ahead to see Whistley Lane.

Cross the road and head down Whistley Lane, which you are now going to follow for about a mile. This is a nice track to walk on and is surrounded by fields and hedgerows which makes for a pleasant and peaceful section.

Cross the road to access Whistley Lane

You will now be away from the centre of the village and also from any busy roads.

At the start Whistley Lane

Oak trees towards the end of Whistley Lane

The track will lead you downhill and past a farm before coming to a dead end, where you will be presented with a farm gate on the left and a small metal gate to your right.

Pass through the small metal gate and you will then cross over a short footbridge. Once over, turn right to pass through another metal gate and you will now be heading in the direction of East Harptree. Looking into the distance you will be able to spot the tower of the church of St Lawrence.

Looking towards East Harptree

You will now walk across two fields with a view towards East Harptree, before arriving at a farm gate with a main road on the other side.

Cross the road and pass through a gate into a small cemetery. Here you need to turn left and walk to the end of the path, where you will see another gate which is the cemetery's main entrance.

There is a small sheltered building just inside the first gateway which has some benches within it, and this is a good place to take shelter if the need arises.

Cross the road and enter the cemetery

The shelter just inside the cemetery

Go through this farm gate on the right

Once through this gate look right and you will be presented with a farm gate, which also has a wooden step for you to use to get over it. Walk uphill now across the field, and towards the top you will see the old stone stile which you used at the start of today's walk to take you on the path around the church of St Lawrence.

Follow this path and you will soon emerge at The Waldegrave Arms and your end point for today – what better place can there be to end a walk!

The stone stile leading past the church to the centre of East Harptree

The Stunning Waldegrave Arms

After the rabbit hunt with cider jugs.
My Great, Great Grandfather is forth from the right –
Fredrick George Aplin
Madgeon Lane, Buckland St Mary 1890

My Grandfather Fred Aplin, quenching his thirst with some cider
after cutting corn in the fields

Hedgers Cider

Hedgers Cider is the creation of Tom Vowles, who is from a traditional farming family which goes back many generations within this beautiful county. Tom's family have lived, farmed and worked around Somerset for hundreds of years, his grandfather was Percy Vowles who made cider at Rocks  Farm in Wraxall - and it was enjoyed by all of the farmworkers, as it was on every farm in Somerset in his day. Tom adds that 'Good Cider makes for good company and good stories - both past and present'.

 Tom started making his delicious cider as a hobby several years ago, and on a small scale for his own personal consumption. However, things have slowly progressed and with a lot of help and encouragement from his wife Jo (and much to the delight of the locals) they made close to 1500 gallons of cider last year – which is an amazing amount for someone who started out just to make his own brew.

Jason Law, proprietor of the Cider Barn in Draycott has shown a great interest in selling Hedgers Cider after trying a variety of their samples, and is now selling a large amount of it to his cider loving customers – which is testimony to the authentic quality of Tom and Jo's farmhouse cider.

All of Hedgers blended cider, which is called 'Mendip Shine' is unsweetened, as are their single variety ciders like - Dabinett, Yarlington Mill, Somerset Redstreak and Ashton Brown Jersey. As Tom sees it 'Cider should not be messed about with or processed in any way', then you can enjoy the true taste of the apple which is what it's all about –

"how can you be a connoisseur of cider if it's watered down, sweetened, carbonated and pasteurised".

Tom also adds that "Most traditionally made cider ferments out at around 6 to 8% depending on the growing season and the sugar content of the apple". There has never been a truer statement, and this is one way of distinguishing between natural, authentic ciders and the mass produced ciders that we often see flooding the market today.

Tom has recently planted over a hundred cider apple trees on his land and aims to plant another two or three hundred, giving Hedgers over twenty different varieties of apple. His aim is to sell Hedgers Cider to local people and supply small local pubs and cider barns - so people will always have traditionally crafted, proper cider which is available to drink and enjoy.

Let's hope that their cider tradition goes on for many generations to come!

Hedgers Cider, Hedgers Hide, Row of Ashes Lane, Redhill, North Somerset, BS40 5TU

Tel: 07768632003

Drinking Cider after a hard day cutting corn
My mother and her sisters are on the left of the photograph

The Awe-Inspiring and Mysterious 'Stanton Drew' which is the third largest complex of prehistoric standing stones in England. If you decide to pay a visit to the stone circle then make sure that you drop into The Druids Arms, it is an excellent pub where they sell a good range of cider, and you will also be able to have your fill of their delicious home cooked food.

Walk 7 - The Blagdon Lake, Leg Thrasher

You will spend the day in a stunning part of Somerset, with some gorgeous views across the picturesque Blagdon Lake. You will have it all on this walk – woodlands, farms, open fields, fantastic views and lots of lakeside areas to sit and take a break.

This is quite a long walk, so if you don't have the time you can turn this into shorter sections to suit your needs – A lovely 2-3 mile walk would be to pick up the first part of what's presented in this book and turn back in the first woodlands that you reach on the north side of the lake, to retrace your steps back to Blagdon.

You will also visit three of Somerset's finest pubs, starting at The Seymour Arms Inn, followed by the The Queen Adelaide, and ending the day at the New Inn which has the most amazing views from its cider-garden.

Approaching Blagdon

(Distance: 7 miles)

Approaching Blagdon you will be treated to some of the most beautiful views that you can lay your eyes on. Pretty villages with their stunning cottages, rich woodlands all around, the odd glimpse down to Blagdon Lake and the amazing Mendip Hill range which lies just to the south of this area. In fact, you will be on the northern slopes of the Mendips which is adorned with lush green meadows and ancient woodlands.

The Seymour Arms Inn - Blagdon

Inside The Seymour Arms Inn

Make your way to The Seymour Arms which is going to be your starting point for today and which is located at the top of Blagdon village (adjacent to the Bath Road or A368). Here you will be able to grab a bite to eat and more importantly get yourself a nice pint of cider from their friendly staff.

Once you are ready to get moving, leave The Seymour Arms, cross over the A368 and walk to your left to head downhill on High Street. On the way down you will find the village shop which is a good place to stock up on any last minute supplies, especially as you won't see another shop for the next few hours.

At the bottom of High Street

At the bottom of High Street you will now have two options:

*   Pop into The Queen Adelaide pub which is only a stone's throw from where you are standing, by tuning left and walking about 50 metres up the road.

*   Turn right and head down the hill towards Blagdon Lake.

1) The Queen Adelaide is a delightful country pub which serves some delicious home cooked food and a variety of local ales and ciders. It is well worth a visit if you have the time to do so, and if you are walking around the lake then this will be your last chance for a drink for a good few hours. If you drop in here, then upon leaving walk back to the bottom of High Street (near the village shop) where you will now turn left to head towards the lake on Station Road.

2) If you opted to just head towards Blagdon Lake you will now be on Station Road which is a very pleasant road to walk along with pretty, bespoke houses all around you. As you descend you will also be able to get the odd glimpse of the lake which you will soon arrive at.

Beautiful Houses in Blagdon

At the bottom of the hill you will have an amazing view out across Blagdon Lake in all of its glory – this is a fantastic sight with the lake

stretching out in front of you, and lush green wooded hills behind it. In fact, Blagdon Lake is a large man-made reservoir which was designed during the late 19th century to supply water to the nearby city of Bristol, and its construction was soon to follow.

Looking across Blagdon Lake

To your left you will also be able to see the impressive sight of the two large water pumping stations that were built back in 1900. The pumping stations are beautiful old buildings and look more like stately homes that are surrounded by a well-established landscaped garden.

You will now need to follow the road over the top of the reservoir's dam which gives you one of the best views of the lake, as the water almost

At the north end of Blagdon Lake's Dam

ends at your feet – and you can see the beautiful Somerset countryside surrounding the lake on all sides, with the Mendip Hills to your right. Incidentally, the dam you are now standing above extends 53 metres below ground level to meet the solid rocks which lie below the valley.

Cross over the dam and on the other side you will see a gate on your right. Pass through the gate and you will now walk on a well-maintained path which will lead you around the western edge of the lake.

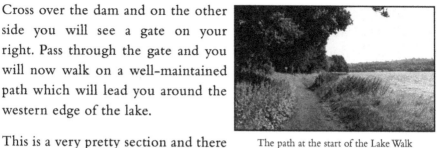

The path at the start of the Lake Walk

This is a very pretty section and there are also a lot of well-placed benches along its length. From the benches you will get clear views out across the expanse of the lake and are good places to stop and have a picnic. You will often see people fishing along the banks of the lake, and sometimes you can see them out in fishing boats bobbing up and down on the water. If you are a keen angler, then this is a good place to revisit – especially if you like catching trout as the lake is full of them and is a good place to practice your fly-fishing.

Looking back across Blagdon Lake to The Mendips

You will also notice that there are tracks leading off to your left up through the adjacent woodland. If you are doing a short walk today then you could go for a stroll through the woods here and then return to the lakeside before making your way over the dam again and back to Blagdon village.

Fly-fishing from a boat

Note: if you are doing this, then once you are back at the village shop on 'High Street' make sure that you turn left down Mead Lane which is located just before the shop. This lane will lead you on a pretty walk past the village church of

Looking north-east across the end of the lake

St. Andrews and over to *The New Inn*, where you can get some delicious food and a pint of cider.

However, if you are walking all of the way around Blagdon Lake then stay on the path which will now lead you to the north side of the lake where you will enter a damp, cool woodland.

Foot bridges in the woods

Views of the lake from the woodland

You will now follow the path through the woods which will also take you across a number of streams via footbridges. This is a nice walk and on the odd occasion you will still be able to get a glimpse out across the lake.

Follow the path uphill and towards West Town, En-route you will leave the woodland to walk on a track that is still surrounded by trees but will have fields to either side of you. Further along you will leave the wooded track to cross an open field, at the other side of which you will go over a stone stile onto a road.

Walking through the old woodland

Cross over the stone stile

Turn left to walk past an attractive house and then turn right at a T-junction to head along a very quiet road with pretty hedgerows on both sides.

Go past this house then turn right

The Wurzels - Somerset Cider Walks 93

After about 10 minutes you will come across a cross-roads, where you will now need to turn right to head down Chapel Hill. You will see where the road got its name from, as just down the hill on your left you will be able to see an old chapel which is now being use as part of a residential

The Old Chapel

settlement – but has a sign on the side of it stating 'The Old Chapel'. Head downhill again and at the bottom you will be able to look to your right and get a wonderful view out over Blagdon lake once again – it would have been a while since you have seen it.

You will now follow Chapel Hill for a while, during which you will pass by Grove Farm then Rugmoor Farm, and the aptly named 'Awkward Hill' which will be a road going off to your left – however, stay on Chapel Hill until you get right to the bottom.

Looking south to Blagdon Lake and The Mendips

Keep your eyes peeled once you are further down as you are looking for the gateway which leads onto a road which enters the lake area – this is easy to spot as it has signs mounted on it from Bristol Water, stating that it is private property and the gate is locked.

Lookout for this gate! Pass through the one on the left hand side!

Note: this is Not the first Bristol Water gate that you come to - see photo above which shows the gate that you are looking for!

To the left of this gate you will be able to see a public footpath sign that will lead you into an open field which you will now have to enter.

If you look to your left after entering the field you will be able to see an old industrial chimney, which looks similar to the type which are scattered all over Cornwall and which were used on the tin mines.

An old chimney stack

Note: the rest of this walk back to Blagdon Village will cross quite a lot of open fields and depending on the time of year can be inhabited by herds of cows. It is worth mentioning in case you have a fear of walking through fields with cows in. If this is the case then it would be wise to do the shorter walk in this book as the only diversion would send you along a busy road with no pathway!

Looking towards the east end of Blagdon Lake

You will now head towards the village of Ubley and will cross a few fields to get there. This is a very scenic section of today's walk with green countryside all around you, The Mendips as the backdrop and the odd glimpse across to Blagdon Lake to your right. *Note: you are now walking around the eastern edge of the lake.*

The 2nd field – aim towards this gate!

At the back of the first field, head towards the opening in the hedgerows where you will find a wooden stile to the right.

Cross the stile and enter the next field – here you need to head to the back of the field on its left hand side where you will find a small wooden kissing gate. Pass through the kissing gate into field number three and walk in a straight line to the back of the field to pass through a metal gate into the last field before reaching Ubley.

Metal gate from field 3 to 4!

Aim for the right hand side at the back of the forth field, and upon approaching the hedgerow you will see a large farm gate which you can now pass through to take you onto (Stilemead Lane).

At the end of the lane you will be 'The Street' - at the end of Stilemead Lane, Ubley at a T-junction where you will need to turn right and walk along 'The Street' where you will pass by the village hall. The Street merges into Frog Lane which you will now follow to its end, where it passes the aptly named Ublcy Farm – there is a public right of way past some of the farms out houses.

Approaching Ubley Farm

Once past the farm you will once again enter the glorious Somerset countryside and will need to cross some more fields. You will be facing west now and will be heading directly towards Blagdon Village – I can vouch that you will now be thirsty and will be looking forward to a nice cold pint of cider and some food. However, there is still a couple of miles to go

On the fields after Ubley

before you arrive at The New Inn in Blagdon.

Go straight across the next few fields. You will find gateways nestled in the hedgerows between each field, but in the summer these can be difficult to spot until you are close to them.

Beautiful scenery En-route to Blagdon

You will then pass by a yoghurt factory where you will walk partly on their land where there is a public right of way, and is signposted to guide you throughout. On the other side of the factory you will be very close to Blagdon village and walking along a lane with fields on either side of you.

At the rear of the Yoghurt Factory

Turn left at this sign to head up to Blagdon

Keep your eyes open for the public footpath sign which points to the right, where you will see a gate which leads through a small wooded area. After the woods you will enter a field, and the path through this field will lead you uphill and back into Blagdon.

Turn right onto Grib Lane at the top of the hill and follow this for a short while before reaching Church Street. Keep following the road round to the right and The New Inn will come into view.

Head uphill across this field to Grib Lane

This is a stunning country pub which serves great food and has a good variety of delicious ciders. The owners and bar staff are very friendly and will lead you out to their amazing cider-garden. This is without doubt one of the best outdoor seating areas of any pub that you will find, with panoramic views across the lake which sits at the bottom of the valley which you are now perched above.

The New Inn - Blagdon

It is stunning here and I can guarantee that you will want to spend some time just relaxing and soaking up the unique atmosphere that The New Inn affords you – so take your time and relax! Note: the owners of The New Inn will take pre-bookings of food orders for walking groups, so if you want

Blagdon lake and valley from The New Inn

to start and end your day here then please contact the owners before arriving, Tel: 01761 462475 . You can then just adjust this walk to suit.

The Church of St. Andrew - Blagdon

After leaving the New Inn it is now a short walk back to the centre of the village and to where you started your day. Come out of the pub and turn left to head towards the church of St. Andrew. There is a lane on the left of the church which you can follow to lead you up to the village playing field. Keep walking along the bottom of the field where you will find a gate which leads onto Mead Lane – at the end of which you will emerge back at the village stores on High Street and where the start of your adventure began.

The view from the lane between the church and High Street

The Aplin family out hay-making and thrashing
at Wetherhayes Farm, Somerset (see below)

Tucker's Grave Inn

No book on Somerset and Cider would be complete without a mention of the world famous Tucker's Grave Inn which lies on the A366, and just outside of the sleepy village of Faulkland (near Bath). Being 1 of only 6 pubs of its type that are left in the country, this 200 year old cider house is on the National Inventory of Historic Interiors, as the inside hasn't changed much since World War 1. Tucker's Grave is what the locals would call a 'proper pub' and

the surroundings are from a by-gone era. Upon entering the Inn you will be greeted by the very friendly staff and locals where you will find that good conversation flows easily, in fact it is so relaxing at this cider house that you may not want to leave its intoxicating atmosphere for some time.

There is no real bar as such, and when you choose your cider it will be poured directly from the barrel as it would have been in the past. Once you have you drink, sit back and relax while taking in the Inn's unique surroundings which include original Georgian wood panelling, a working Victorian fireplace and at the entrance to the 'Tap Room' you will still find an original Georgian, hand-painted door sign. Tucker's Grave also has the most amazing cider garden, so if it's a sunny day head out and enjoy it. On colder days you will be able to warm yourself in front of one of their roaring fires which you can often find a snoozing dog laid out in front of. So, if you find yourself in this part of Somerset, make sure that you pay a visit to the Tucker's Grave Inn to enjoy some of their delicious cider and hospitality.

Tucker's Grave, Faulkland, BA3 5XF
01373 834230

Wassailing at Rich's Cider

Bringing out the Holly Queen

In the orchard
during the ceremony,
sprinkling mulled
cider over the tree's
- to appease the
spirits and ensure
that the next
bumper harvest of
apples is secured!

Toast is also hung
in the apple trees to
present as 'offerings'
to the birds and
spirits. In the past
this was viewed
seriously as a poor
harvest could bring
hunger and famine.

Lightning Source UK Ltd.
Milton Keynes UK
UKHW020225100720
366276UK00009B/316